London

in old picture postcards

by
Ian F. Finlay

European Library - Zaltbommel/Netherlands MCMLXXXV

september 1912, this card in the Valentine's Series, was sent to a convent in Belgium. It shows a fine view of the
..n the direction of its eastern end at the Law Courts. The photo for the card was obviously taken on a fine day
.f both the horse-drawn and early motor bus is full, largely with males wearing straw hats, in common with many of
..ıs. There is also a wide variety of other horse-drawn vehicles and street types. There is a newspaper seller on the left
..ın the right is the archway leading through to the Hotel Cecil which, until the early 1930s, occupied the site of the
.ell-Mex House. It was opened in 1886 and was then the largest hotel in Europe with 600 rooms.

. .. same author:
Bacıış weltliche Kantaten
A Ladybird Book about Stamp Collecting
A Guide to Foreign-language Printed Patents and Applications
Australian Stamp Collecting
Working with Languages
England off the Beaten Track
Translating (Teach Yourself Books)
Careers in Languages

Language Services in Industry
Post and Postage Stamps (Life French Style)
Which Language Shall I Learn?
The Tram and the Postage Stamp
The Trams of Great Britain in old picture postcards
The Trams of London in old picture postcards
The Trams of Wales and the Isle of Man in old picture postcards
The Trams of Scotland in old picture postcards
The Trams of Ireland in old picture postcards

GB   ISBN 90 288 3240 8 / CIP

European Library in Zaltbommel/Netherlands publishes among other things the following series:

IN OLD PICTURE POSTCARDS *is a series of books which sets out to show what a particular place looked like and what life was like in Victorian and Edwardian times. A book about virtually every town in the United Kingdom is to be published in this series. By the end of this year about 175 different volumes will have appeared. 1,250 books have already been published devoted to the Netherlands with the title* **In oude ansichten.** *In Germany, Austria and Switzerland 500, 60 and 15 books have been published as* **In alten Ansichten;** *in France by the name* **En cartes postales anciennes** *and in Belgium as* **En cartes postales anciennes** *and/or* **In oude prentkaarten** *150 respectively 400 volumes have been published.*

For further particulars about published or forthcoming books, apply to your bookseller or direct to the publisher.

This edition has been printed and bound by Grafisch Bedrijf De Steigerpoort in Zaltbommel/Netherlands.

INTRODUCTION

It was Samuel Johnson (1709-84), of dictionary fame, who said that 'when a man is tired of London, he is tired of life; for there is in London all that life can afford.' This view is no less true today than when Johnson expressed it a little over two hundred years ago, although much has changed in London since Johnson's time. The first surviving reference to London is to be found in Tacitus (Annals, Lib. XIV, ch. xxxiii), written in A.D. 115-117 and referring to events in A.D. 61. It is mentioned there as a place notable for its concourse of merchants. The original Londinium has grown vastly in population and area over the centuries. For historical reasons, which need not be considered further here, it has for very many years been *the* centre, not only of Great Britain, but also of the former British Empire and, more recently, of the Commonwealth. This central position contrasts markedly with that of the capitals of such countries as Italy and Germany, neither of which was unified until the second half of the 19th century, this accounting for the relatively many long established centres in them. It was not until the Industrial Revolution in Britain during the 18th century that other large centres, for example Manchester, Birmingham and Leeds, began to develop.

Although very much the centre of Britain, London is by no means a uniform city. It would be more accurate to describe it as a coalescence of a number of previously more or less isolated villages. This development is reflected in the heterogeneous nature of London. It is a city of contrasts at many levels. There are, for example, still the distinct contrasts between London north and south of the Thames which pursues a meandering course through it, those between the West End and East End as well as those within one and the same suburb, for example between the various parts of Kensington and those of Hampstead. These contrasts are, of course, part of the fascination of London, and it is pleasing to find that they have survived some of the less happy efforts of architects and planners in recent decades. The end of World War Two left London with many scars of bombing, virtually all of which have now been healed, in some cases by restoration to a former state, in others by new developments, not always stylistically compatible with their surroundings. Since the 1950s there has also been a vast influx of people from the various parts of the former British Empire, including the present author. Britain's membership of the European Economic Community has also drawn to London many people from other member-countries. Improved means of communication and a general rise in prosperity have also given a major boost to the tourist industry in the past two or three decades. All these, and many other factors, have contributed to changing the face of London as a whole and of many parts of it very drastically over recent years. Happily, this is not the place to assess whether these changes have been for the better or worse. Here it is sufficient to record that they have taken place.

As with most important capital cities, the literature on London is vast, covering every conceivable aspect of the city's history, life and institutions. It has also served as a source of inspiration for artists in many fields, for example novelists, poets, painters and composers, not all of whom were by any means natives of London or even of Britain. Amongst this vast literature in the wider sense are thousands of picture postcards published during the past ninety years or so. These, too, illustrate all aspects of London, its architecture, its parks, its river, its public transport, its street characters, and its many curiosities. As with the picture postcards devoted to any other large city, there is an uneven distribution amongst the cards featuring London in that the areas most frequently visited by tourists have very much more often been chosen as subjects for cards by publishers than some of the less well patronized, but certainly no less interesting parts. It is for this reason that this present selection of picture postcards has sought to combine the better known and less well known aspects of London as they were during the first fifty years or so of the 20th century. The result is a varied, kaleidoscopic picture which will be filled out in greater detail by further volumes in the series devoted to specific areas of London.

All the cards illustrated are from the author's own collection which is, as far as London is concerned, strongest in relation to the development of its public transport system, especially its former trams. The part played by public transport in the development of London, more particularly during the heyday of the picture postcard, should not however be underestimated. Its growth enabled very many working people to live at considerably greater distances from their place of work and in immeasurably more pleasant surroundings. It presaged the age of the commuter. London's present integrated system of public transport also provides the visitor or resident with an excellent vantage point from which to observe the city, i.e. from the top of a double-decker bus, or with an ideal means of getting quickly from A to B, i.e. the Underground. The use of one's own two feet should also not be forgotten as perhaps the very best means of exploring the various parts of London in depth. Interesting views of London can also be obtained from the pleasure boats to be found on the Thames, particularly during the height of the holiday season.

Classification of material is always a problem in a work of this type, covering as it does such a vast and heterogeneous area. It seemed in the end more logical to arrange the cards according to what they showed rather than the part of London represented on them. It proved impossible or impracticable to carry out this principle completely consistently. It is hoped that the occasional 'jumps' will be excused.

The cards are arranged in the following subject order: bridges, buildings, churches, entertainment, gardens and parks, hotels, markets, monuments, museums, palaces, shops, stations, street performers, and street scenes.

As already mentioned, the written literature on London is vast, catering for virtually every specialized interest and taste. Many books have been consulted and recollected in preparing the short texts accompanying the cards illustrated. A few of a more specialized nature or those from the world of fiction are mentioned in the appropriate captions. Two recent works on London have, however, proved so very useful and informative that they deserve separate mention here. They are:

Banks, F.R.: *The New Penguin Guide to London.* 8th edition. London, 1984.

Weinreb, B. and Hibbert, C. (editors): *The London Encyclopaedia.* London, 1983.

Also of relevance are:

Evans, E.J. and Richards, J.: *A Social History of Britain in Postcards 1870-1930.* London, 1980.

Finlay, I.F.: *The Trams of London in old picture postcards.* Zaltbommel, 1983.

1. The river Thames pursues a meandering course through London and is crossed by getting on for twenty road or rail bridges within the Greater London area. The eastern-most and certainly most elaborate of these is Tower Bridge, completed in 1894. Some idea of its fascinating nature can be gathered from the view of it on this card which was printed in France. A section of the Tower of London can be seen between the towers of the bridge. The Tower was begun by William the Conqueror, but has been added to and modified greatly over the centuries. It has served as a prison and is still the place in which the Crown Jewels are kept. Note the paddle-steamer about to pass upstream under the bridge with its funnel lowered. Such steamers used to be popular for excursions to such resorts as Margate.

LONDON BRIDGE AND ADELAIDE HOUSE

2. Until 1749 London bridge was the only one across the Thames in London. It is situated at the river's narrowest point. The bridge shown on this card, published by Raphael Tuck & Sons, was completed in 1831, although its original width of 54 feet was increased to 63 in 1903-4. It was demolished in 1968-71 to make way for a new bridge of pre-stressed concrete. It is 105 feet wide and was completed in 1972. The demolished bridge has been re-erected at Lake Havasu City in Arizona. Adelaide House was completed in 1924 and is occupied by shipping offices. The top of the Monument (cf. card No. 52) can be seen above the left corner of Adelaide House. London bridge is a fine vantage point from which to view London east and west of it.

BLACKFRIARS BRIDGE, LONDON.

10492-2   ROTARY PHOTO E.C.

3. Published by the Rotary Photographic Co. Ltd., and posted to an address in Switzerland in September 1911, this card shows a fine view of Blackfriars bridge. It was built in its present form between 1860 and 1869 in which year it was opened by Queen Victoria. It was widened on its west side in 1907-10 from 70 to 105 feet, this being the form in which it appears on this card. It was one of several bridges in London to be crossed by trams. Because of its width, the trams could be segregated from the rest of the traffic. That in the foreground of the card is bound for Norbury in South London. Note the wide variety of horse-drawn vehicles on the bridge, including open-topped buses. There is also a solitary cyclist in front of the tram. Blackfriars station and railway bridge can be seen to the right of the road bridge. To its left can be seen the dome of St. Paul's Cathedral.

LONDON, ST. THOMAS'S HOSPITAL AND WESTMINSTER BRIDGE.

4. Completed in 1862, Westminster bridge was one of the main thoroughfares for trams across the Thames. This card shows no fewer than ten trams on the bridge and its northern approach. Of interest is the mixture of single- and double-deck cars. The former used the Kingsway subway, completed in 1908, until it was enlarged to take double-deck cars in the early 1930s. The subway formed the only direct tramway link between south and north London. The large complex of buildings on the card is St. Thomas's Hospital. It was opened by Queen Victoria in 1871. Its design was approved by Florence Nightingale who established there the Nightingale Training School of Nursing, thereby revolutionising the profession. The hospital was severely bombed in World War Two and has since then been largely rebuilt. In 1982 the hospital had close on a thousand beds.

Scotland Yard, Thames Embankment, London

5. Published in the Valentine's series, this card shows the north side of Westminster bridge (cf. card No. 4). It is of interest from many points of view. In the central foreground is the statue of Boadicea, a British queen in the time of the emperor Nero. It was made in the 1850s and unveiled in 1902. Prince Albert is said to have lent the horses as models. The imposing building on the left is (New) Scotland Yard, the former headquarters of the Metropolitan Police Force. They were moved to Broadway and Victoria Street in 1967. Two trams, one with an open, the other with an enclosed top, can be seen about to turn onto Westminster bridge. Note the space between the two rails for current collection, since overhead wires were not permitted for this purpose in central London. Charing Cross or Hungerford railway bridge can be seen in the right background. It was completed in 1864 and incorporated a footbridge. Finally, note the small building to the right of the statue advertising boat trips to Greenwich.

Barracks.   Chelsea.

6. Situated in Chelsea Bridge Road were Chelsea Barracks, designed by George Moore for 1,000 footguards and built in 1861-62. The rather gaunt looking building, as shown on this card, was completely rebuilt in a modern style by Tripe and Wakeham in 1960-6 and provides quarters for regiments of the Guards' Division. Chelsea Barracks were not the only ones to be rebuilt in modern times. Knightsbridge Barracks were demolished in 1966 and rebuilt in the form of a huge tower block designed by Sir Basil Spence overlooking Hyde Park. They are the headquarters of the Household Cavalry with accommodation for over 500 men and almost 275 horses. The card was sent in the latter part of the Edwardian era from an address in South London to one in Maida Vale in North London and contains the rather cryptic sentence: 'will write later on when I know what I am for.'

The County Hall, London.

7. Published in the 'National' series of Millar & Lang Ltd., Glasgow, this card shows the eastern end of St. Thomas's Hospital at the southern end of Westminster Bridge (cf. card No. 4) with, on the other side of the southern end of the bridge, County Hall. Begun in 1912, this impressive building was opened in July 1922 by George V. It has subsequently been added to greatly. Originally the headquarters of the London County Council, which came into being in 1889, it is now those of the Greater London Council. The site was previously occupied by wharves, timber yards and factories. During excavation of the site the remains of a Roman boat were found, these now being stored in the Museum of London. One wonders what the solitary female figure on the Embankment (cf. card No. 5) is thinking.

BIG BEN AND THE HOUSES OF PARLIAMENT. LONDON.

8. Opposite St. Thomas's Hospital on the northern side of the Thames are the Houses of Parliament, a fine view of which can be seen on this card. Part of the hospital can be seen in the left background across the river. The Houses of Parliament incorporate a number of sections with distinct functions, for example the House of Commons, the House of Lords, the Speaker's residence and a variety of libraries. The eastern end of the complex is dominated by the clock tower which houses the great bell of 'Big Ben', cast in 1858 and weighing over 13.5 tons. It was named after Sir Benjamin Hall, First Commissioner of Works when it was hung. The western end of the complex is dominated by the Victoria Tower. The present Houses of Parliament were erected over a period of years from 1840, the first parliament there having been opened by Queen Victoria in 1852. Various parts of the complex are open to the public at appropriate times.

9. Radio broadcasting was started by the British Broadcasting Company at Savoy Hill, between the Strand and Victoria Embankment, in November 1922. Expansion was such that new premises were soon needed, and a site was found at the corner of Langham Place and Portland Place to the north of Oxford Circus. This was in 1928, and the rather ugly building, resembling a battleship, was occupied in 1932. Over its main entrance is a sculpture of Prospero and Ariel, one of the last works by Eric Gill and chosen by him as a symbol of broadcasting. The white building was painted grey during World War Two, but this did not prevent it being bombed. It is still the headquarters of the British Broadcasting Corporation (B.B.C.), although this admirable body has very many other buildings scattered throughout London, including the Television Centre at Shepherd's Bush.

B.B.C. London

Y.W.C.A. CLUB, GREAT RUSSELL STREET, LONDON, W.C.1.

10. Situated in Great Russell Street, not far from the British Museum, is the central club of the Young Women's Christian Association. It was established in 1887 by the amalgamation of two organizations, both of which started in 1855, one of which was a hostel for Florence Nightingale's nurses en route to and from the Crimea. The building in which the central club is housed was built in 1931 and was designed by Sir Edwin Lutyens. In addition to its residential facilities, it also has an excellent small concert hall in which the present author heard many chamber music concerts in the early 1950s. Almost opposite the Y.W.C.A. central club is the new building of the Young Men's Christian Association which contains over 750 bedrooms, a large sports and recreation complex, and a conference centre. It was opened in 1976, replacing the memorial building to Sir George Williams, who founded the Y.M.C.A. in 1844. The card is in the 'Kingsway' series published by W.H. Smith & Son.

The Guildhall, London.

11. The City is that part of London which is richest in tradition. Amongst its best known buildings in this context is the Guildhall, the Hall of the Corporation of the City of London and the seat of municipal government in the City. It is the principal place of civic assembly. The present hall, part of which is shown on this card, was built in 1411-25. The building was severely damaged in the Great Fire of 1666. It was also damaged during the great fire of 29 December 1940, but has long since been restored and extended. Associated with the complex of buildings constituting the Guildhall are also the Guildhall Art Gallery, consisting mainly of 19th century British paintings, and the Guildhall Library which is particularly rich in works on London. The southern approach to the complex from King Street is that shown on the card.

UNILEVER HOUSE, BLACKFRIARS BRIDGE, LONDON. 132

12. Postally used a few weeks before the outbreak of World War Two, this card in the 'Excel' series is of interest in that it shows the headquarters of one the country's largest industrial firms, i.e. Unilever, on the northern side of Blackfriars bridge (cf. card No. 3). The site now occupied by Unilever House, used to be that of De Keyser's Royal Hotel. It opened in 1874. It is interesting to note that the hotel catered for Guildhall (cf. card No. 11) banquets. It was also patronized by travellers arriving at and departing from Blackfriars station. It was closed after World War One, and Unilever House was built on the site in 1930-31. When the photo for this card was taken trams were still using Blackfriars bridge. One can be seen to the left of the bus on route 76 having Victoria station as its destination. Note that there are still a few horse-drawn vehicles.

AUSTRALIA HOUSE, STRAND, LONDON.

13. Postally used in August 1928, this card shows a fine view of the entrance of Australia House. Built between 1912 and 1918, it is still very much the first port of call for most Australians arriving in London. Flanking the entrance are figures representing Exploration and Agriculture, while the cornice is occupied by 'The Horses of the Sun'. The interior of the building is embellished with Australian wood and marble. The card is also of interest for the excellent views of two open-topped buses, both on line 11 which still runs from Shepherd's Bush to Liverpool Street. Also on the card are several early cars and horse-drawn vehicles. Note, too, the policeman on the road at the extreme lower right of the card.

LAW COURTS, LONDON

14. At the eastern end of the Strand, a few hundred yards from Australia House (cf. card No. 13) are the Law Courts or, more accurately, the Royal Courts of Justice. They were opened in 1882 and are a good example of Victorian Gothic architecture. The whole complex of buildings has a frontage of more than 500 feet to the Strand. It contains more than 1,000 rooms and about 3.5 miles of corridors! The main purpose in building it was to have a centre in which all civil cases could be dealt with. Criminal cases are heard in the Central Criminal Courts (cf. card No. 15). This card was published by E.B. Horwood & Co., Ltd., London. It is also of interest in that it shows two horse buses waiting outside the courts. Note, too, the underground Ladies' Cloak Room, another typical feature of London.

CENTRAL CRIMINAL COURTS, LONDON.

10484—9

15. Built in the Edwardian era, between 1902 and 1907, the Central Criminal Court was on the site of the former Newgate Prison in front of which public executions took place from 1783 until 1867. Thereafter they were carried out within its walls until 1901. The present building, opened by Edward VII in 1907, is known familiarly as the Old Bailey after a street in its vicinity. The building was severely damaged by bombs in 1941, but has since been restored. It was also extended considerably in 1972. The height from the ground to the head of the statue of Justice on the dome (not visible on this card) is 212 feet. Since it was opened many notorious criminals have been tried and convicted in the Old Bailey, including Dr. Crippen (1910), William Joyce ('Lord Haw-Haw') (1945) and Peter Sutcliffe, the 'Yorkshire Ripper' (1981). This card was published by Wm. Whiteley, Ltd., London. Note the double-deck horse bus on the left of the card.

16. During the middle and latter part of the 19th and early part of the 20th century many large blocks of so-called 'dwellings' were built in various parts of the inner London area, in many cases by the London County Council, established in 1888 as successor to the Metropolitan Board of Works. The L.C.C. was in turn superseded by the Greater London Council in 1965. The L.C.C. had very wide powers, including responsibility, with the 28 Metropolitan Borough Councils, for housing. Several of its blocks of dwellings are still standing and in use. Their modern counterpart are high-rise blocks of flats built mainly in the 1960s. Many of the former, including the block in Swan Lane shown on this card, are as gaunt as the latter are unsightly. Swan Lane is on the north side of the Thames very near to London bridge. Other similar dwellings can still be seen in Clerkenwell, in some of the streets off Kingsway and in parts of south London near the Thames.

17. In the latter part of the 19th and early years of the 20th century there were many disputes in the London docks. As a result of a Royal Commission on the subject, the Port of London Authority eventually took over full control of the tidal river and its docking in 1909. The Authority was first housed in a building in Trinity Square overlooking the Tower of London. It was built between 1912 and 1922. It was described by the art historian Nikolaus Pevsner as 'a lasting monument to Edwardian optimism like a super-palace for an international exhibition, showy, happily vulgar and extremely impressive.' It was sold in 1971, and the P.L.A. moved to smaller offices in the World Trade Centre at St. Katharine Dock. The card was published by John Beagles & Co. Ltd., one of the pioneers amongst publishers of photographic cards. Also in Trinity Square is Trinity House which is entrusted with erecting and maintaining lighthouses, lightships and other seamarks.

651.S. PORT OF LONDON AUTHORITY OFFICES. LONDON. BEAGLES' POSTCARDS
THIS MAGNIFICENT EDIFICE IS SITUATED IN TRINITY SQUARE.
OVERLOOKING THE TOWER OF LONDON.
THE ARCHITECTURAL DESIGN OF THE BUILDING IS CONSIDERED TO BE
ONE OF THE FINEST IN LONDON.

LONDON. NORTH ENTRANCE BLACKWALL TUNNEL.   Copyright. G. D. & D. L.

18. Not only are there several bridges across the Thames (cf. cards Nos. 1-5), but also several tunnels under it. These latter are intended in part for the London Underground and in part for motor vehicles. Readers particularly interested in this subject may like to refer to Nigel Pennick's 'Tunnels under London', published by Fenris-Wolf, Cambridge, in 1980. There are two road traffic tunnels under the Thames, namely Rotherhithe tunnel, running from Shadwell to Rotherhithe and built between 1904 and 1908, and Blackwall tunnel, running from Blackwall to Greenwich, the northbound section of which was built between 1891 and 1897. The card illustrated here was published by Gottschalk, Dreyfus & Davis, a very prolific London firm of card publishers. It was printed in Germany prior to World War One. The elaborate northern entrance to the tunnel shows that even purely utilitarian structures were considered important enough to be given some character. The same principle applied to the entrances to many railway tunnels.

London "The Zoo" — Monkey House

19. Published by the Excelsior Fine Art Publishing Co., London, this card shows a delightful view of the monkey house in the grounds of London Zoo in Regent's Park. The Zoological Society of London was founded in 1826, and its collection of animals was opened in 1828. Since then the zoo has developed and expanded greatly. It also has an open-air section at Whipsnade. Over the years many new buildings have been erected for the various categories of animals. The monkey house on this card has been replaced by a much more modern, but far less charming looking building or pavilion in the last few years. Many of these modern buildings were designed by Sir Hugh Casson. London Zoo is very popular, not only with natives of London, but also with tourists. It is also a major centre for zoological research and many rare animals have been kept there in recent years, for example the giant panda, a native of China.

St. Andrew's Hospital, Dollis Hill, N.W.

20. London has a very large number of hospitals of both a general and specialized character. Many of them date from the 19th or early part of the 20th century. Their interiors and the facilities they offer are, however, in most cases very much more modern than their external appearances suggest. This card, published by W. Stackemann & Co., Teddington, London S.W., was printed in Saxony, as were large numbers of pre-1914 British and American cards. It shows a view of St. Andrew's Hospital in Dollis Hill in the north-western part of London. Dollis Hill station on the London Underground was opened on 1 October 1909 and contributed in no small way to making the area popular for and accessible to commuters. Since then it has grown to become just another of London's north-western suburbs. The hospital was opened in 1913 and is typical in appearance of many other medium-sized hospitals of the same era scattered throughout London. At least its surroundings are quieter and more rural than those of St. Thomas's Hospital (cf. card No. 4).

656

ST. PAUL'S CATHEDRAL, LONDON

21. There must be several hundred churches within the Greater London area catering for the spiritual needs of a multitude of different faiths. In this context the Central London Mosque with a dome 75 feet high and a minaret of 150 feet, built close to the Islamic Cultural Centre in Regent's Park in 1978, must be one of the most colourful. It is reminiscent of the mosque near the Rue Monge in Paris. Compared with many European cities, London has relatively few buildings in the baroque style of architecture. One is however St. Paul's Cathedral, shown on this card. It stands on the site of a mediaeval church which was burned down in the Great Fire of 1666. The present church was begun in 1675 and completed in 1710. It is regarded as the masterpiece of Sir Christopher Wren (1632-1723), and is, to some extent, reminiscent of the Karlskirche in Vienna in appearance. The card shows the extent to which St. Paul's was hemmed in by surrounding buildings prior to World War Two.

22. As mentioned in the Introduction, London – as well as many other parts of Britain – suffered greatly as a result of bombing in World War Two. This involved not only severe loss of life, but also damage to buildings. St. Paul's Cathedral was miraculously spared in the great fire of 29 December 1940, which destroyed a large area around it, as can be seen from this card. It did, however, receive hits from high-explosive bombs which damaged the high altar and destroyed much of the glass in the north transept. It contains the tombs of and monuments to many famous Britons, for example the Duke of Wellington, Dr. Samuel Johnson, Lord Nelson and the painters Sir Joshua Reynolds and J.M.W. Turner. It was in 1981 the scene of the wedding of the Prince of Wales and Lady Diana Spencer. The card was published by the Photochrom Co. Ltd., London and Tunbridge Wells, one of the country's most prolific postcard publishers.

Limehouse Church, London, E.

23. Published by the firm of Frederick Hartmann, credited — rightly or wrongly — with the introduction of the 'divided back' postcard in 1902, this card shows a view of Limehouse Church in Commercial Road in the East End of London. The writer of the card describes it as 'a present from the East End'. It was printed in Saxony and therefore dates from before World War One. The church of St. Anne Limehouse was built between 1712 and 1724 and was consecrated in 1730. It was designed by Nicholas Hawksmoor (1661-1736), one of the most original English baroque architects. It was gutted by fire in 1850, but repaired in the following seven years at a cost of £13,000. In common with so many buildings in the East End, it was damaged by bombing in 1941. Its clock is the highest church clock in London. The district of Limehouse takes its name from the lime kilns or oasts known to have been there from the 14th century.

CHURCH ROW.

HAMPSTEAD LONDON.

24. Hampstead is one of the most attractive parts of London and it has over the decades been the chosen place of residence of many of the city's artists, musicians and writers. Amongst its most delightful streets is Church Row, shown on this card. The Row consists of terraces of 18th century dwellings. At its end is St. John's Church, the parish church of Hampstead. It was built in its present form between 1744 and 1747 by John Sanderson. Buried in its churchyard are such famous people as John Constable, George du Maurier, Sir Walter Besant and Sir Herbert Beerbohm Tree. Part of the church was threatened with demolition in 1874-75, and opposition to this led to the establishing by William Morris of the Society for the Protection of Ancient Buildings in 1877. Happily both the church and the Society are still flourishing almost a century later!

The Oratory, South Kensington

25. Published in Valentine's series, this card shows a fine view of the Oratory in South Kensington, better known as Brompton Oratory. It is a Roman Catholic church served by a congregation of secular priests of the Institute of the Oratory, founded by St. Philip Neri in Rome in the late 16th century. The Institute was introduced into England by Cardinal Newman in 1847. The church was completed in 1884 being in Italian baroque style and designed by Herbert Gribble. The dome, 200 feet above the floor to the top of the cross, was added in 1896. On the left of the Oratory on the card can be seen a statue of Cardinal Newman who died in 1890. Also visible on the card is at least one hansom cab and the cabmen's shelter outside the Oratory. Although the former has disappeared, the latter is still there. Further north along Brompton Road is Knightsbridge with its fashionable shops, including Harrod's.

WESTMINSTER CATHEDRAL, LONDON

26. Published in Valentine's 'Colourtone' series, this card shows Westminster Cathedral, situated near the south-east end of Victoria Street. It is the main Roman Catholic church in England and was designed by John Francis Bentley in an early-Christian Byzantine style, inspired partly by St. Mark's in Venice. It was described by the writer Hesketh Pearson as being of the 'later marzipan period' in relation to style! Be this as it may, it is a striking building with its alternate bands of red brick and Portland stone. The square campanile is 284 feet high to the top of the cross. The cathedral opened for services in 1903 and was consecrated in 1910. It was also the setting in June 1903 for the first London performance of the oratorio 'The Dream of Gerontius' composed and conducted by Edward Elgar. The present Archbishop is Cardinal Basil Hume, who succeeded Cardinal Heenan in 1975.

27. In common with all large capital cities, London offers a wide variety of facilities for entertainment and relaxation, although the pattern of these has changed over the decades. Gone for the most part are, for example, many music halls so popular in Victorian and Edwardian times. Many cinemas, too, have disappeared during the past thirty years or so, some having been converted into bingo halls! London still has its pubs however, and most inhabitants of the city have their favourites amongst them or even their very own 'local'. Shown on this card, published by Charles Martin and printed in Germany prior to World War One, is a famous 16th century tavern, 'The Spaniards', situated in Hampstead (cf. card No. 24). To the left of the inn is a restored 17th-century toll house. Two other well-known inns in the vicinity are 'Jack Straw's Castle' and the 'Old Bull and Bush', the latter having been made famous by a music-hall song. 'The Spaniards' was patronized by such literary figures as Shelley, Keats and Byron.

Aldwych from the Strand, London.

28. There are many tourists who come to London with a main aim of visiting the many theatres it contains. These, too, are regrettably liable to be closed and demolished, this having befallen the Gaiety Theatre shown on this card in the 'National' series, published by Millar & Lang Ltd., Glasgow. There had long been a Gaiety Theatre at the east end of the Strand. That shown on this card was opened in October 1903 in the presence of Edward VII and Queen Alexandra. After many successful productions, it closed in February 1939 and was eventually demolished in 1957. The site it once occupied is now taken by Citibank House. In its heyday it had many distinguished managers, including Oscar Asche and C.B. Cochran. Jack Hulbert and Cecily Courtneidge also enjoyed many successes in the theatre. At the other end of the island of buildings between Aldwych and the Strand is Australia House (cf. card No. 13). Also visible in the left background of the card is the Waldorf Hotel, built between 1906 and 1908. Note, too, the open-topped buses passing the theatre on the card. Those interested in the history of the theatre will see that 'The Last Waltz' was being performed in the Gaiety when the photo for this card was taken.

Royal Albert Hall, London

29. Prior to the building of the Royal Festival Hall, opened in 1951, the year of the Festival of Britain, London was distinctly short of concert halls. The Queen's Hall, in Langham Place, was destroyed by bombing in 1941, necessitating the moving of the Promenade Concerts to the Albert Hall, where they are still held. Popular for recitals and chamber music were (and still are) the Wigmore Hall in the street of that name and Conway Hall in Red Lion Square. This card, sent from London to an address in Berlin in January 1914, about 6 months before the outbreak of World War One, shows the Royal Albert Hall which was opened in 1870 by the then Prince of Wales. Its name commemorates that of the husband of Queen Victoria, who died in 1861, ten years after he had done so much to inspire the Great Exhibition of 1851. Although not noted for its acoustic properties, the Royal Albert Hall has been the scene of many memorable musical and other performances. It is on the fringes of museum-land in South Kensington, and opposite to it is the Albert Memorial (cf. card No. 55).

12033

The Maze, Hampton Court Palace.

30. Inspection of a map of the Greater London area will reveal a surprising number of green sections, the majority of which is gardens or parks. There are in fact no fewer than 387 parks in London more than 20 acres in size! Their number and distribution are features very highly prized, not only by residents, but more particularly by visitors to the capital. It would easily be possible to fill a book with descriptions and cards of the major London parks, as has H. Davies in 'A Walk round London's Parks', London, 1983. I have, however, preferred here to concentrate on the smaller and less well-known gardens and parks. This card, published by Gale & Polden, Ltd., London, presents a view of the maze in Hampton Court Gardens. The site was purchased in 1514 by Thomas Wolsey, a year before he became cardinal. The maze was constructed for William and Mary towards the end of the 17th century. It will be recalled that it plays an important part in one of the episodes in Jerome K. Jerome's novel 'Three Men in a Boat', which appeared in 1889.

LONDON. THE PAGODA, KEW GARDENS.   Copyright.

31. The Royal Botanic Gardens, popularly known as Kew Gardens, date from the 18th century, if not earlier. They combine in an ideal way, as does the London Zoo (cf. card No. 19), science and art, the former in that they house important collections of flora from all parts of the world, the latter in that they enable the public to enjoy many of these in their natural environment. Amongst the many interesting features of these gardens is the Pagoda, depicted on this card in the Star series, published by Gottschalk, Dreyfus & Davis, London. It was printed in Bavaria, this betraying its pre-World War One origin. The pagoda is a replica, four-fifths natural size, of a famous Japanese gate, 'The Gateway of the Imperial Messenger' of Chokushi-Mon. It was presented to the gardens by the Kyoto Exhibitors' Association after it had been displayed at the Japanese-British Exhibition held in Shepherd's Bush in 1910.

A BUSY SPOT ON
HAMPSTEAD HEATH.

32. Hampstead Heath, described as the finest 'lung', in the neighbourhood of London, was acquired by the London County Council (cf. card No. 7) between 1871 and 1927. It is situated in the north-eastern part of the suburb of Hampstead and covers just under 800 acres in all. Hampstead has for many decades been one of the most favoured of London suburbs and has been the home of numerous artists, intellectuals and professional people, not least because of its proximity to the Heath. The Heath comprises several sections or parts, and includes in its northern section Kenwood House, the home of a magnificent collection of paintings, including one by the Dutch artist Vermeer. Fairs are still held on Hampstead Heath at Easter and on Bank Holidays. Attendances of up to 100,000 have been recorded on a Bank Holiday. This early 20th century card gives some idea of the crowds and atmosphere on Hampstead Heath on one of these occasions. A much quieter corner of Hampstead can be seen on card No. 24.

Finsbury Park — The Lake   London

Tuesday

Dear Agnes,
J. & I at Tennis Monday, had a ripping
time and tea. Please come to-morrow
call for me about 2 o'clock.   love Hilda

33. Published by Stengel & Co. of Dresden and Berlin, this undivided back card, postally used in May 1902, shows a delightful view of the lake in Finsbury Park in north-east London. The park is 115 acres in extent and was one of the first of London's municipal parks, having been opened in 1869. The cost at that time was £472 per acre! Finsbury Park is now a very much less quiet and peaceful part of London than that suggested by the scene on this card. It is, however, scenes like this that illustrate just what an unexpected city London is. There is no better way of experiencing this than to travel from one terminus to the other of some of the bus routes which cross London either from west to east or north to south or vice versa. The message on the card is also of interest. I wonder how many people would today entrust to a postcard a request for a visit on the day after it was sent!

1262 Entrance to the woods. Winchmore Hill.

34. Reference has already been made to the important role played by public transport in extending the boundaries and thereby increasing the population of London. The card illustrated here is yet another example of this process which was taking place in the latter part of the 19th and early part of the 20th century. It was postally used in March 1908 and published by Gordon Smith, 15 Stroud Green Road, near Finsbury Park (cf. the preceding card). The view on the card is of the entrance to the woods at Winchmore Hill on the northern outskirts of London. Prior to the coming of the railway in 1871 it was a remote hamlet. It was before and after World War One swamped by middle-class suburban housing such that it is now just another residential area in North London. How much more peaceful and attractive was this part of it in the middle years of the Edwardian era.

Flower Beds, Plashet Park, East Ham.

35. Published in the Wilbro series of Wilson Bros. and printed in Prussia, thus indicating its pre-World War One production, this card shows a charming scene in one of London's smaller parks, namely that known as Plashet Park in East Ham in the eastern part of London. In addition to a number of parks, this area also accommodates a number of cemeteries, including the City of London Cemetery and the Manor Park Cemetery. Closely associated with what was originally the hamlet of Plashet was the Quaker family of Frys, the best-known member of which was probably Elizabeth (1780-1845), one of the main promoters of prison reform in Europe. Plashet House in which the family lived from 1784 to 1928 has since been demolished. Many of those depicted on this card were obviously posing for the occasion, including the gentleman with the white beard mowing the lawn, but the result is a delightful vignette dating from Edwardian times.

CLISSOLD PARK.

302.

36. Published by Charles Martin, London, and posted from Stoke Newington to an address in Islington a mile or two away in February 1905, this card shows a section of Clissold Park, situated in Stoke Newington, a little to the south-east of Finsbury Park (cf. card No. 33). The park, 54 acres in size, is traversed by the New River and also contains a notable villa of about 1830. It was opened by Lord Rosebery in 1889 and named after an eminent Swedenborgian curate who had worked in the neighbourhood in the early 19th century. Clissold Park is yet another example of those many smallish parks scattered around London, often in the least expected areas. They are in many ways relics of the time when what is now Greater London consisted of a number of more or less isolated villages which have since coalesced into a rather heterogeneous whole.

A COSY NOOK, GOLDERS HILL PARK.

37. The area known collectively as Hampstead Heath has been added to extensively over the years, and this card, produced more or less locally by E.W. Schröder of Childs Hill, shows a section which was added to it in 1899 at a cost of £38,000. It is Golders Hill and is situated in the western section of the Heath near Manor House Hospital and the 'Bull and Bush' public house, famous from the song performed by Florrie Ford. The pub itself dates from 1645. Golders Hill is said always to have had the finest flower garden in the whole of the Heath. It also contains a deer and animal enclosure, a bandstand, ponds and tennis courts. The card, sent to Territet in Switzerland in March 1913 shows a quiet corner or 'cosy nook' in the park. Note the drinking water fountain in the centre of the picture.

38. Very much in the centre of London are St. James's Park and the Green Park, the latter in particular being surrounded on two sides by some of the capital's most famous buildings, including Clarence House, the home of Queen Elizabeth, the Queen Mother, and the Treasury. Also very much in the neighbourhood are Downing Street, in which is the official residence of the Prime Minister, and the Cenotaph in Whitehall. This card, printed in France, shows part of the lake in St. James's Park with, in the background, the War and Foreign Office. Once again, one is struck by the semi-rural appearance and atmosphere of an area a few hundred yards from the hustle and bustle of London's main shopping centres. Although the scale is quite different, one is reminded of the Jardin du Luxembourg in Paris or even of the Begijnhof in Amsterdam.

LONDON,- ROTTEN ROW

39. Hyde Park, 360 acres in size, has been described as the People's Park. It certainly is compared, for example, with St. James's Park (cf. the preceding card) in that it has its Speakers' Corner and has often formed the assembling point for marches through London for a variety of causes. Situated at the southern part of Hyde Park is Rotten Row, perhaps originally 'Route du Roi'. It is about a mile in length and was laid out as a sandy track in 1690. It is reserved for horse-riders, and the paths on either side of it used to be favourite meeting-places for the fashionable after church on Sunday mornings. This card, published by the London Stereoscopic Co. in its 'Lesco' series, shows part of Rotten Row as it used to be. Several horse-riders can be seen on the Row with the occasional cycle, horse-drawn carriage and early motor car on the road adjoining it. Note, too, the number of people observing the riders. The view would be very different today.

The Dog's Cemetery, Hyde Park, London.
F. K. 1581.

40. Published by F. Kehrhahn & Co., Bexley, to judge from the initials on its front, this card shows a section of the north-eastern part of Kensington Gardens, bordering on the north-western part of Hyde Park, almost opposite Lancaster Gate underground station, known variously as the Pets' Cemetery and Dogs' Cemetery. The caption on the card could be said to be wrong on two counts in that the location is given as Hyde Park and the apostrophe would suggest that merely one dog was buried in the cemetery. Be this as it may, the first burial took place there in 1880, being that of the favourite dog of the Duchess of Cambridge, wife of the then Ranger. It soon became fashionable for pets — not only dogs, but also cats, monkeys and birds — to be buried in this little cemetery. By 1915 there were over 300 small gravestones, several of which are visible on the card. The cemetery is now full and the area it occupies is fenced off. This cemetery is reminiscent of that for dogs at Asnières to the north-west of Paris.

10481-6   TEMPLE GARDENS, LONDON.   ROTARY PHOTO. E.C.

41. Published by the Rotary Photographic Co. Ltd., possibly the most prolific publisher of 'real photograph' postcards, this card is labelled as showing the Temple Gardens. It would seem, however, more accurately to be showing part of the Victoria Embankment Gardens because of the presence and position of the Hotel Cecil (cf. cover picture). This hotel occupied, until its demolition in the early 1930s, the site now taken by Shell-Mex House. Next to it, to the right, is the Savoy Hotel which is still operating and likewise has its main entrance in the Strand. Most of the area from Villiers Street eastwards along the northern bank of the Thames is occupied by gardens, at least until as far as Blackfriars Bridge, those nearer this bridge being more accurately described as the Temple Gardens. They take their name from the Temple, a complex of buildings occupying an important place in the country's legal system. Note the bandstand in the left of the gardens. This was a very typical feature of many late Victorian and Edwardian parks and gardens.

42. It is by no means merely London north of the Thames which is endowed with so many delightful parks. Posted from London to an address in Duisburg in Germany in July 1913, this card shows one of the entrances to Dulwich Park in south-east London. Its extent is 72 acres and it was opened in 1890 by Lord Rosebery, the first chairman of the London County Council, established in 1888 as successor to the Metropolitan Board of Works (cf. card No. 7). The park has facilities for boating and is noted for its azaleas, rhododendrons and rockery. The notice on the gate states that 'The speed of motor vehicles must not exceed 8 miles an hour.' Dulwich is also famous for a picture gallery and a boys' school, Dulwich College. Both these institutions are located near to Dulwich Park. The area is a popular residential suburb in south London.

Brockwell Park.

43. A little to the north-west of Dulwich Park, in the district called Herne Hill, is Brockwell Park. It is 127 acres in extent and was opened in 1892, likewise by Lord Rosebery (cf. the preceding card). It is interesting to note that it was largely due to the local authorities that funds were set aside for providing this park because of the large amount of residential building in Herne Hill and Brixton (to the north) in the 1880s. The park is particularly noted for its old English garden, a section of which is shown on this card which was postally used in May 1910. It is worth noting that very many of the parks and other attractions of London illustrated in this book could be reached by the many trams which ran in London in the early decades of the 20th century. An 'Official Tramways Guide', covering services operated by the London County Council, was published in 1911 specially for the coronation of George V and Queen Mary. It ran to 186 pages, was illustrated with pictures and route maps and cost one old penny! I am ashamed to say how much I paid for a secondhand copy about two years ago.

44. Although situated on the north shore of the Thames in North Woolwich, it seemed appropriate to place this delightful card of the Royal Victoria Gardens here rather than amongst those of other parks north of the river. The park is barely ten acres in extent and was opened in 1851. The park is relatively difficult of access which is unfortunate since it is so attractive, as can be judged from this card in the Valentine's series, although published by a local firm, i.e. H. Pryce & Son, Woolwich. The writer of the card, postally used in August 1909, says that she went to the park on Sunday evening to listen to the band playing and that there were thousands of people there. Note the two statues on either side of the pathway and the policeman with his white beard. There is not a sign of litter either!

Cook's Orchard, Bostall Wood, Plumstead   Valentines Series

45. Another card in Valentine's series is the final example of a London park or, more accurately in this case, a heath and wood, namely Bostall Heath and Woods extending over a little more than 130 acres in Plumstead in south-east London. The area was acquired for the public in the 1890s. The heath and the woods are separated by Bostall Hill Road. To the immediate north-east is Abbey Wood. The whole area is on the eastern fringes of Greater London south of the Thames. In the good old days of London trams the Heath and Woods were served by route 34 as was Abbey Wood. The card shows Cook's Orchard which was situated in part of Bostall Wood.

LONDON, HOTEL GREAT CENTRAL.

46. There are hundreds of hotels in Greater London, ranging in size from those with fewer than ten rooms to those with several hundred. The spread of the railways in the middle and latter part of the 19th century accounted for the building of many large hotels near the main London railway termini. Several of these are still in use and many were originally built by the railway companies having stations near them. Some are however no longer functioning as hotels, for example that shown on this 'Silverette' card, published by Raphael Tuck & Sons. It was postally used in January 1913. The hotel in question was the Great Central, built opposite Marylebone Station in the road of the same name. It was opened on 1 July 1899 and had 700 rooms. It was requisitioned for wounded soldiers in 1916 and again in World War Two. It became the headquarters of the British Railways Board in 1982. Note the open-topped horse bus on the extreme right of the card.

IMPERIAL HOTEL
Russell Square, LONDON.

47. The area around Russell Square in Bloomsbury contains very many hotels. It is relatively near at least three of the railway stations carrying passengers from the north of the country to London, as well as being within walking distance of the British Museum and several West End theatres; hence its popularity with tourists. The Imperial Hotel shown on this card was built in red brick with terracotta ornaments in Russell Square between 1905 and 1911. It was designed by C.F. Doll, who was also responsible for the Russell Hotel. The Imperial was famous for its Turkish baths of glazed Doulton ware. The building was demolished in 1966 and the new Imperial Hotel was opened in June 1969. It has about 450 bedrooms.

ROYAL HOTEL, LONDON.

48. Many of the larger London hotels built in the late Victorian and Edwardian era were highly ornate in style (cf. cards Nos. 46 and 47), this no doubt reflecting the role of London as the centre of a huge empire 'on which the sun never set'. Most of the large hotels of more recent decades have been very much more functional in appearance, some even resembling army barracks (cf. card No. 6). A good example of this type is shown on this card, being the Royal Hotel situated in Woburn Place, north of Russell Square in the direction of Euston Road and the three large terminal stations, i.e. Euston, St. Pancras and King's Cross. Also of interest on the card, probably dating from the early 1930s, are the two buses, one with its open stairs leading to the covered upper deck, the other still with a completely open upper deck on which the conductor can be seen collecting fares. Note, too, the two horse-drawn vehicles. Would that Woburn Place were as quiet today as on this card!

Smithfield Market.

49. London has many markets, some of which are very large and centralized in relation to various categories of goods, while others are of a more generalized and local character. A major 'growth area' in recent years have been the many antique markets scattered throughout the capital. The market shown on this card is however very much more down to earth. It is the main entrance to the London Central Meat Market, popularly known as Smithfield. The building shown on the card was opened in 1868, and further extensions were made in 1875 and 1899. Smithfield is situated in the City of London, a little to the north of St. Bartholomew's Hospital, the oldest in London. Smithfield market sells more than 350,000 tons of meat annually. It also has its own public house which is licensed from 6.30 a.m. The horse-drawn vehicles visible on the card have however long since disappeared.

50. The Sunday morning street market in Petticoat Lane (renamed Middlesex Street in about 1830) has long been a favourite, not only with Londoners, but also with visitors to the city and, regrettably, also with pickpockets! Situated near Aldgate at the fringe of London's East End, it has since Victorian times been a street market specializing in all kinds of second-hand goods. It has in recent years expanded into the surrounding streets so that fish, birds and reptiles are now sold there. It started as an old clothes market at the beginning of the 17th century. The part of London in which it is situated was settled in by many Huguenot weavers from France and Jews from Eastern Europe. The card shows predominantly an area with old clothes. Note the preponderance of males and the variety of their headgear. Also of interest are the many advertisements and notices on the buildings.

Do you know where this is. George.

COLUMBIA MARKET, BETHNAL GREEN

51. Over the years many of London's markets have either disappeared completely or have been moved away from the city centre. The latter has been the case with Covent Garden, London's best known fruit and vegetable market, moved to Nine Elms in Battersea, south of the Thames, in 1973. Columbia Market in Bethnal Green, shown on this card published by W. Straker, Ludgate Hill, has however now disappeared completely. It was conceived and financed by the philanthropist, Baroness Burdett-Coutts, as an attempt to wean costermongers from the streets. Designed in an elaborate Gothic Style, it was opened in 1869, but did not prove successful. It was ultimately let as workshops and finally demolished in 1958. In its heyday bells in the clock tower sounded a hymn tune every quarter-hour. A flower market is now held near the original site in Columbia Road. The market building is reminiscent of the ornate style of many of London's hotels of roughly the same period and looks more like an Oxford or Cambridge college than a market in the East End!

The Monument, London.

52. It would be surprising if a city with as many historical associations as London did not have many monuments and statues. One of the oldest must be that commemorating the Great Fire of London which started on the night of 2 September 1666. It destroyed 87 churches, 44 livery halls and no fewer than 13,200 houses, although it is said that only nine lives were lost. There are vivid accounts of it in the diary of Samuel Pepys. It was not until 1672 that life and trade had returned more or less to normal in the area affected. The Monument, shown on this card published by J.J. Samuels Limited in the 'Arcadian' series, was designed by Sir Christopher Wren and was built between 1671 and 1677 to commemorate the Fire. It is a fluted Doric column 202 feet in height and is situated near the north end of London Bridge (cf. card No. 2). Because of suicides, the gallery was enclosed by a cage in the 1840s.

The Marble Arch, London.

53. Based on the Arch of Constantine in Rome, Marble Arch was erected in 1827 and was originally placed in front of Buckingham Palace. It was in 1851 moved to its present site at the north-east corner of Hyde Park, allegedly because it was too narrow to admit the state coach. It was islanded in 1908 and must now be passed by several thousand vehicles a day. Only senior members of the Royal Family and the King's Troop Royal Horse Artillery may pass through it. It is very near the site of Tyburn Gallows, used for public executions for 500 years until 1759. Note the traffic policeman on the card and the fine horse-drawn carriage about to pass him.

Nelson Monument, Trafalgar Square.

54. Surely London's best-known square is Trafalgar Square with the Nelson monument at the top of its column in its centre. The column was erected between 1839 and 1842. The stone statue of Nelson, 17 feet high, was raised in the following year. The four bronze lions at the foot of the column were designed by Landseer. They were not placed in position until 1867. The square is surrounded by a number of well-known buildings, two of which can be seen on this card, i.e. the National Gallery in the left background and the church of St. Martin-in-the-Fields on the right. The building with the globe on its top to the immediate right of the column is the Coliseum Theatre in St. Martin's Lane. It became in 1968 the new home of the Sadler's Wells Opera Company after having been used as a cinema for seven years. Trafalgar Square itself is a popular site for demonstrations and celebrations.

55. Opposite the Royal Albert Hall (cf. card No. 29) is the Albert Memorial. It was erected between 1863 and 1876 to a design by Sir George Gilbert Scott as a national monument to Prince Albert, the consort of Queen Victoria, who died in 1861. Below the monument's canopy is a seated figure of the prince, holding the catalogue of the Great Exhibition of 1851 which was very largely his idea and 'child'. The lower sections of the memorial are lavishly decorated with reliefs of artists and men of letters of every period, groups representing Agriculture, Commerce, Manufactures, and Engineering, and at the outer corners of the steps groups symbolizing the continents of Europe, Asia, Africa, and America. Opinions have varied greatly over the years about the aesthetic merits of the Albert Memorial. Suffice it to say that it remains virtually unique amongst London's many memorials.

The Albert Memorial, London.   G. W. Beamand, London.

Cleopatra's Needle, London.

56. Although the Monument is the earliest memorial to be erected in London which is illustrated in this book, there is another which is immeasurably older in origin. It is Cleopatra's Needle to be found on the Thames Embankment between Hungerford railway bridge and Waterloo bridge. It is a granite monolith nearly 60 feet high and weighing over 180 tons which was cut from the quarries at Aswan in Egypt in about 1475 B.C. and was transported down the Nile to be erected at Heliopolis. It was then moved to Alexandria in about 12 B.C. It ultimately toppled over into the sand and was there when it was presented to England by the Turkish Viceroy of Egypt. It left Alexandria in September 1877 and eventually reached London in January 1878 after many adventures. The 'needle' bears various inscriptions in hieroglyphs. Buried beneath it on the Embankment are various everyday objects dating from the time it was erected there.

LONDON. Wellington Statue and Arch

57. This undivided back card, printed in Saxony, was postally used in June 1905, having been posted from Dorking in Surrey to Durban in Natal. It shows one of the several statues of the Duke of Wellington to be found in London, namely that at Hyde Park Corner. The bronze figure of the duke is seated on his favourite horse, Copenhagen. There are bronze figures of soldiers of various regiments at each corner of the polished granite plinth. The statue was erected in 1888. To the right of the statue is the Wellington Arch, designed by Decimus Burton in 1828. To it was added in 1912 a large bronze four-horse chariot with a figure of Peace, which does not appear on this card which predates it. Of interest on the card is the horse-drawn bus with the advertisement for Ogden's cigarettes on its side and the lady pushing a pram to the left of the gentleman in the top hat. Hyde Park Corner is today London's busiest traffic centre.

58. One of the focal points in London's West End must surely be the statue of Eros or, more accurately perhaps, the Shaftesbury Memorial Fountain, situated in the centre of Piccadilly Circus. The money for it came from public donations, and it was intended to be in memory of the 7th Earl of Shaftesbury, a great philanthropist. It was the first London statue to be cast in aluminium and was designed by Alfred Gilbert. It was unveiled in 1893 by the Duke of Westminster. From 1922 to 1931 it stood in the Embankment Gardens while the underground station was being excavated. During World War Two it was kept at Egham in Surrey. Up till then it had for many years been a favourite place for cockney 'flower girls' to congregate with their wares. It is today, regrettably, often the meeting-place of far less salubrious characters. To judge from the female fashions, the representation of the statue on this card dates from the early post-war years after it had been returned from Egham to its original home.

ADMIRALTY ARCH

59. Published by Raphael Tuck & Sons Ltd., this real photograph card shows a fine view of Admiralty Arch, taken from the Mall and looking in the direction of Trafalgar Square and the Strand. The Arch was built in 1910 and was designed by Sir Aston Webb as part of the Queen Victoria memorial scheme. The structure consists of three identical arches, each with wrought-iron gates, although those of the central arch are opened on ceremonial occasions only. The Mall, originally laid out in about 1660 is a straight and wide thoroughfare which is ideal for the ceremonial processions for which it is so often used. Note the Latin inscription above the arch referring to 1911, the tenth year of the reign of Edward VII, and the affection in which his mother, Queen Victoria, was held by the ordinary people. The whole structure reflects the splendour of Edwardian times when the British Empire was at its height.

S 14954.   PETER PAN STATUE, KENSINGTON GARDENS, LONDON, W.

60. London is rich in literary associations as readers of the works of Charles Dickens and Sir Arthur Conan Doyle will be only too well aware. There was in fact published in 1970 a book by P. Roberson on 'The London of Charles Dickens'. Visitors walking around London will also have noticed the many blue plaques on buildings indicating that famous literary figures once lived in them. This card, published by W.H. Smith & Son in the 'Kingsway' series, shows yet another literary association in the form of the Peter Pan statue in Kensington Gardens. Peter Pan was the motherless boy 'who would not grow up' in Sir James Barrie's play of that name, which was produced in 1904. The statue was commissioned by Barrie from Sir George Frampton, and it was unofficially arranged with the Commissioner of Works where it should be erected. The site became an immediate tourist attraction from 1912. Below Peter blowing his pipes are many other human and animal figures, some of which can be recognized on this card.

91791 J.V. The Cenotaph (by Night), London

61. World War One saw the end of an era, not only in Great Britain, but also throughout Europe and, in many cases, beyond it, since it was also a war involving very many men and women from distant parts of the Empire such as Australia, New Zealand and Canada. Very many places – large and small – throughout Britain have their war memorials, more often than not listing the names of those from them who lost their lives in the war. Few families remained unaffected, directly or indirectly, by it. The Cenotaph in Whitehall, shown here by night on this Valentine's card, was designed by Sir Edward Lutyens and was first used for the anniversary of Armistice Day on 11 November 1920. It was inscribed 'To the Glorious Dead'. This dedication now covers those of both world wars. The Cenotaph is adorned merely by the flags of the three services and the Merchant Navy. There is a service in front of it every year on the Sunday nearest the 11 November at 11 a.m., accompanied by a two-minute silence.

NURSE CAVELL STATUE, ST. MARTIN'S PLACE LONDON

62. The section on monuments concludes with another memory of World War One. The card shows the marble statue of Nurse Edith Cavell, by Sir George Frampton (cf. card No. 60), which was erected in front of a high granite background in 1920. This nurse, whose last words were 'Patriotism is not enough', was shot by the Germans in Brussels in October 1915. Born in Norfolk in 1865, she became matron of a medical institute in Brussels in 1907. During the war she helped English and French soldiers to reach the Dutch frontier. In August 1915 she was arrested and imprisoned by the Germans and, despite numerous efforts to obtain a reprieve, was shot together with one of her assistants, on October 12 of that same year. In May 1919 her body was removed to Norwich Cathedral. To the left of the statue, which is in St. Martin's Place, is the National Portrait Gallery. The building with the globe on the right is the Coliseum Theatre (cf. card No. 54).

WEST GATE, ROYAL NAVAL COLLEGE, GREENWICH.

220061.

63. London probably has as many museums as any other major European capital. They cover all manner of objects from paintings through furniture and costumes to musical instruments. Although referred to as the Royal Naval College at Greenwich, the complex of buildings on this card, published by Valentine & Sons Ltd., was erected between 1696 and 1752 from the plans of Sir Christopher Wren. The building accommodated naval pensioners from 1705 to 1868, this accounting for the name Greenwich Hospital under which it is also known. In 1873 it became a Royal Naval College for training officers, as it is described on this card. Also in the complex is a museum containing, amongst other things, mementoes of Nelson and a model of the battle of Trafalgar. The Painted Hall in the complex contains a gallery of about 200 naval pictures. Also in the vicinity is the National Maritime Museum which presents a survey of naval history from Tudor times to the present. There are many other items of naval interest in and around Greenwich, including 'Gypsy Moth IV', the boat in which Sir Francis Chichester made his single-handed voyage around the world in 1967.

BRITISH MUSEUM, LONDON.

64. Situated in the centre of Bloomsbury in Great Russell Street (cf. card No. 10) is the British Museum. Although it has been said that everything in it seems designed to instruct, not to delight, its collections are outstanding in their own field, and cannot be neglected. The museum originated from an offer by Sir Hans Soane, who died in 1753, that Parliament should buy his collection of antiquities and works of art. His offer was accepted and, after many moves, the collection was eventually housed in the building shown on this card in Valentine's 'Photo-Brown' series. It was designed by Robert Smirke and completed in 1847. The museum contains several very well-known items, including the Elgin marbles, two of the four extant copies of Magna Carta, Captain Scott's diary, and a large collection of Egyptian antiquities, including various mummies. Also at present situated in the British Museum is the Reading Room of the British Library, although it is not part of the Museum (cf. card No. 65).

The Reading Room.

65. The central section of the complex of buildings forming the British Museum in Great Russell Street (cf. card No. 64) is occupied by the Reading Room. It is not part of the museum, but has, since 1973, been one of the three parts of the British Library, the other two being the National Central Library and the National Lending Library for Science and Technology, situated at Boston Spa in Yorkshire. The Reading Room was built between 1852 and 1857. Over the decades it has been used by innumerable scholars from all parts of the world. Amongst its best-known users have been Thomas Carlyle, George Bernard Shaw, Karl Marx and Vladimir Lenin. It is not open to the public, and those wishing to use it have to obtain a reader's ticket. This is normally issued to those who cannot carry out their specific line of research elsewhere. The library is one of the four entitled to receive a copy of each new publication in Britain. Shortage of space has long been a problem, and a new site for the library has been found near St. Pancras Station in Euston Road. It is scheduled for completion in 1991. This card shows a section of the Reading Room with its central section and rows of desks radiating out from it.

THE IMPERIAL INSTITUTE, LONDON

66. South Kensington has come to be known as 'museum land', since it is the site of several large museums, including the Natural History Museum and the Victoria and Albert Museum. The fascinating building on this card, the Imperial Institute, used also to occupy a site in this part of London. It was built between 1887 and 1893, being opened in that latter year by Queen Victoria whose jubilee in 1887 it was intended to commemorate. It housed a permanent exhibition of the products of the various parts of the British Empire. This function has now been taken over by the Commonwealth Institute which has, since 1962, occupied new premises in Kensington High Street. All that now remains of the Imperial Institute building is the central tower, the remainder having been demolished when the Imperial College of Science was expanded. This latter institution was established in 1907 'to give the highest specialised instruction and to provide the fullest equipment for the most advanced training and research in various branches of science, especially in its application to industry'. It became a school of the University of London in the following year.

HORNIMANS MUSEUM, DULWICH

67. Not all London museums are situated in its centre, that shown on this card, published by E.A. Schwerdtfeger & Company, with their trade mark 'EAS' in a heart-shaped figure, being in south-east London in Forest Hill, a little to the east of Dulwich Park (cf. card No. 42). It is the Horniman Museum, founded by F.J. Horniman, head of the well-known tea firm. He assembled a large general collection on his travels abroad, which was originally housed in his home, Surrey House. This house was demolished in 1898 and replaced by the Art Nouveau style building on the card. It is constructed of stone and red brick and has a distinctive clock tower. Also associated with the museum is a park, the whole complex covering 21 acres. Horniman presented it to the London County Council (cf. card No. 7) as a gift to the people of London. The museum contains a wide variety of exhibits and is particularly famous for its collection of musical instruments. When the present author last visited it, he was able to reach it by tram, an example of which can be seen on this card. Note, too, the solitary cyclist and the horse-drawn vehicle on the left. Altogether a delightful card with many personal memories.

ST. JAMES'S PALACE, LONDON. (308)   43701

68. London is well endowed with palaces and royal residences which date from the 15th to the latter part of the 19th century. Postally used about three months before the outbreak of World War Two, this Valentine's card shows the entrance to St. James's Palace, situated in Pall Mall. It was formerly a leper hospital, but was rebuilt by Henry VIII in 1532. It is in fact the oldest of the royal residences in London. Although it has not been used by the sovereign for a long time, other than for levees and other ceremonies, it is still the nominal headquarters of royalty, and the British Court is diplomatically called the 'Court of St. James's' to which foreign diplomats are accredited. Both Queen Victoria and her grandson, the future George V, were married in St. James's Palace. It was also where Elizabeth II made her first speech as queen in February 1952.

London. Kensington Palace from Gardens.

69. Bordering on the western perimeter of Kengsinton Gardens (cf. cards Nos. 40 and 60), is Kensington Palace. The view of it on this card, published by W. Straker Ltd., London, in fact shows it as seen from the Gardens. It was formerly Nottingham House and was sold by the son of the first Earl of Nottingham to William III, who added a further storey to the building, based on designs by Sir Christopher Wren. William III died there, as did Queen Anne and George II, the last sovereign to reside in the palace. Queen Victoria was born in the palace on 24 May 1819, as was the later Queen Mary in 1867. There are apartments in the palace for various members of the Royal Family.

Marlborough House   London

70. Printed in Dresden and published by Stengel & Co., this undivided back card shows another royal residence in London. Situated in Pall Mall (cf. card No. 59), it is Marlborough House, which was built by Wren in 1710 for the Duke of Marlborough. It has subsequently been enlarged and modified. After the death of Edward VII, it was the residence of Queen Alexandra. It likewise became the residence of Queen Mary, the consort of George V, from 1936 until her death in 1953. It was in 1962 renovated as a Commonwealth conference and research centre. The building also houses a reference library of books on Commonwealth subjects, and has a public information office on the ground floor. Certain parts of Marlborough House are open to the public from Easter to the end of July.

BUCKINGHAM PALACE - LONDON

71. Bearing the initials 'R.A.' as a trade mark, this card was published by Radermacher, Aldous & Co., and shows a front view of Buckingham Palace. The palace takes its name from Buckingham House, built between 1702 and 1705. It was purchased from the Duke of Buckingham for George III in 1761. It subsequently passed to George IV who commissioned John Nash to remodel it in 1824. After the accession of Queen Victoria in 1837 it became the permanent residence of the sovereign in London. Several members of the present Royal Family have also been born in it. The Palace is situated at the western end of the Mall which runs from Admiralty Arch (cf. card No. 59) to it. Behind the Palace are extensive gardens. The interior of the Palace is never open to the public. When the Queen is in residence the Royal Standard, her personal flag, flies at the palace's masthead. In front of the palace, visible on the right of the present card, is the Queen Victoria memorial, sculptured by Sir Thomas Brock, with Sir Aston Webb as architect, and completed in 1911. Her seated figure can be seen on it looking in the direction of the Mall.

S 14946   LAMBETH PALACE FROM RIVER THAMES, LONDON, S.E.I.

72. Published by W.H. Smith & Son in their 'Kingsway' series, this card shows a fine view of a palace on the south side of the Thames. It is Lambeth Palace, the official residence of the Archbishop of Canterbury. The buildings were begun by Archbishop Hubert Walter (1193-1205), although Stephen Langton (1207-28) was the first archbishop to live there. The palace has been greatly modified over the centuries, but still retains its essentially mediaeval atmosphere and appearance. Parts of the complex were damaged by bombing in World War Two. The complex is also the place where the Lambeth Conference of Anglican bishops is held every ten years. The last was held in 1978 and was attended by more than 300 representatives from Britain, the Commonwealth, and the United States. The complex also houses an important ecclesiastical library which is open to accredited persons on application. Opposite the palace on the northern side of the Thames are the headquarters of Imperial Chemical Industries Plc., formed in 1926 through the amalgamation of various separate chemical manufacturing companies. Imperial Chemical House was built by Sir Frank Baines between 1927 and 1929.

Crystal Palace, London

73. Published in Valentine's series, this card shows a panoramic view of the impressive Crystal Palace at Sydenham in south-east London. Its history goes back to the Great Exhibition of 1851, the brain-child of Prince Albert, husband of Queen Victoria (cf. card No. 55). The structure, constructed from 4,000 tons of iron and 400 tons of glass, was designed the building Joseph Paxton, superintendent of the Duke of Devonshire's gardens at Chatsworth in Derbyshire. After the exhibition the building was removed from Hyde Park and re-erected at Sydenham. It was enlarged, and outside there were fountains, supplied by the two water towers visible on either side of the main building on this card. Also in the grounds was a collection of plaster casts of prehistoric animals. The building caught fire during the night of 30 November 1936 and was destroyed. Only the prehistoric animals survived and can still be seen in Crystal Palace Park. Ironically, the 'Paleis voor Volksvlijt', built in Amsterdam at the instigation of Dr. Samuel Sarphati and opened on 16 August 1864, suffered the same fate. Modelled on London's Crystal Palace, although much smaller and very different in design, it caught fire during the night of 17-18 April 1929 and was likewise for the most part destroyed.

Tram Terminus.

74. This card shows a close-up view of the central section of the main Crystal Palace building, but seen from the opposite side to the previous card. After its removal from Hyde Park the palace was used, amongst other things, as a concert hall. Justifiably famous were the Saturday afternoon concerts given there in the winter season and conducted by August Manns from 1855 to 1901. Associated with them were the annotated programmes prepared by Sir George Grove from 1856 to 1896. They are models in their genre and can still be read with profit today. This card is however of interest mainly in that it shows one of the open-top trams of the South Metropolitan Electric Tramways and Lighting Company Ltd., at the Crystal Palace terminus. Note the advertisements for at least two still well-known products on the top of the tram. Note, too, that in this part of London, well away from the centre, trams were permitted to collect their current from an overhead wire, a method prohibited in the central parts for aesthetic reasons.

75. Situated in Muswell Hill in north London, Alexandra Palace, visible in the background on this card, was north London's rival to the Crystal Palace (cf. cards Nos. 73 and 74). It was opened in May 1873 as the reconstructed international exhibition building of 1862. It was named in honour of Princess Alexandra, Princess of Wales. In spite of valiant efforts the palace never rivalled the Crystal Palace in popularity in spite of the number of facilities it offered. Part of the building was acquired in 1936 by the British Broadcasting Corporation for television studios. Regular transmissions began in November of that year. In October 1955 the first experimental colour television tests were carried out there. A year later the B.B.C. Television Centre was moved to Shepherd's Bush, but the palace was still used for recording Open University television programmes. Much of the building was destroyed by fire in July 1980. The building and grounds are still used for various events, for example antique fairs and sporting events. From the early years of the century until the 1930s a tram route, operated by Metropolitan Electric Tramways, ran to the palace ground. It was unusually, for London, operated by single-deck cars.

OLD CURIOSITY SHOP. LONDON

76. Greater London contains thousands of shops catering for every need both conventional and unconventional. In some cases, particularly in Central London, there are streets or areas specializing in specific goods, for example books or antiques. There are also special directories to London's shops in these two categories of goods. The shop shown on this card, in the 'Kingsway' series of W.H. Smith & Son, is situated in Portsmouth Street off Kingsway on the left quite near Aldwych (cf. card No. 13). It is said to be the oldest shop in London having been built in about 1567. It is alleged to be the home of Little Nell in Dickens' novel 'The Old Curiosity Shop', which was published in 1841, although other sites, for example, near the present National Portrait Gallery, seem more likely contenders for the honour. The shop shown on the card sells gifts, antiques and mementoes and no doubt makes the most of its alleged connexion with Dickens and his heroine. It will be recalled that Oscar Wilde said that one would have to have a heart of stone to read the death of Little Nell without bursting out laughing!

OXFORD STREET. LONDON. "SELFRIDGE'S."

77. Oxford Street is surely London's busiest shopping street, not least because it is the site of the main branches of many of the city's department stores. Its only competitor in this respect would be the slightly less crowded Regent Street and the much more sedate Knightsbridge area. Situated at 400 Oxford Street at its corner with Portman Street is Selfridge's Ltd., the largest store in London. It was founded by an American, Harry George Selfridge. He was backed in his desire to open a store in Oxford Street by Sam Waring of Waring and Gillow, on condition that he did not sell furniture. His Oxford Street store was opened on 15 March 1909. It was built to an American design. Selfridge retired in 1940 and in 1952 the store was bought by Lewis's Investment Trust and Charles Clore of the British Shoe Corporation. It is still noted in particular for its window displays at Christmas. The view of it on this card dates from a time when Oxford Street was very much less crowded and far more pleasant than it is today.

VICTORIA STATION   A361/1124

78. Reference has already been made to the major role played by public transport in the development and expansion of London as the country's capital. Foremost in this development were the railways which may be classified into three categories in the London context, namely those bringing passengers from various parts of the country to the capital, those serving the capital's suburbs, and the trains of the London Underground. All these categories gave rise to different types of stations, most of those bringing passengers to London from afar being associated with large hotels, usually owned by the relevant railway company. This card, sent from London to Antwerp in July 1913, shows an interesting view of the entrance to London's Victoria Station, dating from the early 1860s. Victoria has always been the major station for boat trains, and this is reflected by the signs on both sides of the station entrance. Note, too, the horse bus and collection of horse-drawn cabs in the station forecourt and the early open-top motor buses and early car in the road outside the station. Bus route No. 2 still passes the station today. The hotel associated with Victoria Station is the Grosvenor.

Charing Cross and Strand, London

79. Charing Cross Station was opened in 1864. It is situated in the Strand at its western end (cf. the cover picture which shows a view of the Strand a few hundred yards further eastwards). The station was the London terminus of the South Eastern Railway. The Charing Cross Hotel above it was built at the same time as the station. In front of the station stands the Eleanor Cross. When Edward I's wife, Eleanor of Castile, died in Nottinghamshire in 1290 he had crosses erected at the 12 places at which the funeral cortege had rested on its way to Westminster Abbey, and that in front of the station is a replica of the last of them before the Abbey. Apart from the disappearance of the 'Bureau de Change' the station looks very much the same today as it does on this card. On the other hand, road traffic in the Strand is immeasurably greater and there are no longer any horse-drawn vehicles. The card is in the Valentine's series.

The Station   Thornton Heath

80. Railways, either as part of the suburban network or as part of the Underground system, have given birth to the commuter and had a major influence on the development of new residential areas radiating in all directions from the centre of London. This was also the case with Thornton Heath which is situated between Norwood and Croydon in south London. Its railway station, shown on this card, printed in Saxony and postally used in November 1904, was built in 1862 and gave rise to some residential development, although this did not really get underway until the introduction of an electric train in 1901. In this case the station was also passed by an electric tram route having its terminus at Purley slightly further south. Note the very elaborate lamp standards and the conductor collecting fares on the open top of the tram.

High Street & Tube Station, Clapham Common.

81. Printed in Prussia and published locally, this card shows a view of Clapham Common underground station at the corner of High Street and Clapham Park Road in south-west London. The station was that of the City & South London Electric Railway. It is stated that it offered the quickest route to the West End, the journey to Chancery Lane taking 24 minutes and that to the British Museum 26 minutes. I doubt if the present times to these two destinations would be much shorter. The Underground station serving the British Museum was opened in 1900 and closed in 1933. It can still be seen between Holborn and Tottenham Court Road on the Central Line. Also typical of many Underground stations is the shop selling cigarettes and cigars attached to them. That on the card, to the right of the station entrance, was run by F. Hudson. Note, too, the open-top tram approaching the station along High Street. Clapham Common station was opened on 3 June 1900.

Copyright.

82. Published by Gottschalk, Dreyfus & Davis in the 'Star' series and sent to an address in Simla in India in the early years of Edward VII's reign, this card shows a view of Shepherd's Bush station in the western part of London. It is stated on the station that the fare is 2d to any station, in other words the 'tuppenny' tube. Nowadays it is mainly in East European countries that we find very cheap public transport with a flat fare system instead of the highly complicated and elaborate system now in force in London. In common with many stations on the London Underground system Shepherd's Bush had two different lines running through it, as it still does today, i.e. the Metropolitan line and Central line. The Central line station was opened on 30 July 1900, and the Hammersmith & City line (now on the Metropolitan line) on 13 June 1864. The station shown on the card is that on the Central line. Note, too, the open-top London United Electric Tramways' car, running between Shepherd's Bush and Uxbridge, further to the west, outside the station. There is another version of this card on which the advertisements on the front and side of the tram have been altered to those referring to the card's publisher!

7.   LONDON LIFE : An Entertainer escapes from a bound sack in Charing Cross Road.

83. London in the late 1980s is in many ways a far less colourful and interesting city than it was even in the early 1950s. Amongst the colourful elements which have virtually completely disappeared are the variety of street performers and entertainers. These used to include a variety of musicians, pavement artists, escapologists and others. There used, for example, to be every Saturday afternoon in Great Russell Street near the Y.W.C.A. club (cf. card No. 10) an old man with a barrel organ. I suppose in earlier years he would have had his monkey with a tin in which to collect any donations. Occasionally one finds music students performing in shop doorways in the evenings or playing for theatre queues. Some are sometimes found in the passages of the Underground, but their talents are mostly restricted to strumming a few chords on a guitar. This card in Charles Skilton's series of 'London Life' shows a crowd very passively watching an escapologist about to emerge from a bound sack while his assistant looks on. The photo for the card was taken in the early post-war years, to judge from the men's and women's fashions. The location for the performance was Charing Cross Road, now filled with a very different looking crowd.

1.   LONDON LIFE: Costermonger " Pearly Kings and Queens " in Southwark. *Photo: G.P.U.*

84. Costermongers are basically people who sell fruit, vegetables, etc., from barrows in the street. They have been part of the London street scene for centuries and some appear in Shakespeare's plays. Costermongers were regarded as the élite amongst the street vendors. The name comes from 'costard', a large ribbed apple, and 'monger', meaning 'dealer' or 'trader' and turning up in other words such as 'fishmonger'. Being unlicensed, costermongers could not expect legal protection, so each borough chose its own 'king' to protect their rights. These resulted in the 1880s in the pearly kings and queens, so-called because of their clothes which are studded with pearl buttons. Their association was founded in 1911, and they now devote their time to a variety of charitable activities. This card, also in the 'London Life' series of Charles Skilton, shows a group of costermongers in Southwark, a borough just south of the Thames to which both London and Blackfriars bridges (cf. cards Nos. 2 and 3) lead.

LONDON—LUDGATE HILL, FROM FLEET STREET.

85. The last and largest category of old picture postcards of London presented here is devoted to street scenes. They have not been chosen because of specific buildings or monuments, but to show where people lived, worked and shopped as well as, in many cases, how they travelled about in the days before most people had their own car. There has been some attempt to arrange the cards according to the part of London represented on them. This card in the 'Lesco' series of the London Stereoscopic Company was postally used in February 1907. It shows a very congested Ludgate Hill, looking in the direction from Fleet Street, a continuation of the Strand, in the direction of St. Paul's Cathedral which can be seen in the centre background of the card. Fleet Street was, and still to some extent is, the centre of the newspaper world, as is evident from the names on the windows of the buildings on the right. Note the number and variety of horse-drawn vehicles and the steam from a train crossing the railway bridge leading to Holborn Viaduct station.

لوندره ساحة

80 LONDON. — Cheapside. — Looking West. — i▯.

86. Printed in France, this card shows a good view of Cheapside looking west. On the left is part of the Mansion House, the official residence of the Lord Mayor of London. The spire which can be seen in the centre background is that of Bow Church, famous for the peel of its bells. They were destroyed by bombing in 1941. It is said of a true cockney that he will have been born within the sound of Bow Bells. The Mansion House is situated at a busy junction in that Cheapside radiates from it in the direction of Holborn and the West End, while Queen Victoria Street leads down to the left from it to reach the Thames at Blackfriars bridge (cf. card No. 3). Also in this area is the Bank of England and the Stock Exchange. Note, once again, the large number and variety of horse-drawn vehicles, including open-top buses. On the back of the card there is an advertisement for a French bookshop off Leicester Square. It is described as 'un coin de France en Angleterre'.

Holborn Circus, London.

87. Published in the 'National' series of Millar & Lang Ltd., Glasgow, this card shows another important junction of no less than six streets. It is Holborn Circus which was constructed in 1872. This part of London is very near Staple Inn and Smithfield Market (card No. 49). One of the smaller streets leading from Holborn Circus is Hatton Garden, the centre of the diamond trade in London. The bronze statue in the middle of the Circus is of Prince Albert who is raising his hat to the City of London. It was erected in 1874, made by Charles Bacon and was presented to the City of London. It cost £2,000. Note, yet again, the variety of horse-drawn vehicles and the many men in bowler or top hats, no doubt 'city gentlemen' of their time.

S 14947   L.C.C. TRAM SUBWAY FROM SOUTHAMPTON ROW TO THE
THAMES EMBANKMENT SHOWING KINGSWAY IN THE
BACKGROUND, LONDON, W.C.2.

88. Although London could hardly be referred to as a planned city and has certainly never been subject to the degree of deliberate clearance and reconstruction which resulted in the boulevards of Paris or the 'Ringstrasse' in Vienna, it is in fact traversed between Aldgate in the East (cf. card No. 50) and Marble Arch in the West (cf. card No. 53) by one continuous thoroughfare, some sections of which we have already seen in the last two cards. The next important junction on this thoroughfare after Holborn Circus is that with Kingsway running south to Aldwych (cf. card No. 13) and Southampton Row running north towards Euston Road. Kingsway was itself not opened until 1905. It was formed by demolishing many slums. There was built below it between 1905 and 1906 a subway for single-deck trams which rendered possible through running from the Embankment and South London to North London. The subway was enlarged in the early 1930s to take double-deck cars. A single-deck car can be seen ascending from the subway on its way to North London. Note the roughly 50/50 mixture of horse-drawn and motor vehicles on this card, probably dating from the middle 1920s.

Tottenham Court Road, London.

89. Progressing westwards from Aldgate to Marble Arch, the next important junction after Kingsway is to be found where Tottenham Court Road proceeds to the north and Charing Cross Road to the south. This junction is shown on this card with Tottenham Court Road in its centre. Of interest in particular are the three open-top buses, their tops being covered with a variety of advertisements. Prior to the formation of the London Passenger Transport Board in 1933, there had been various companies operating buses in London. The main one of these was the London General Omnibus Company, one of whose buses can be seen in the centre of the card, while that on the right is one operated by a different company, as evidenced by the 'National' on its side. Note the tall building on the right in Tottenham Court Road with the letters 'Y.M.C.A.' on it. The building was constructed in 1912, but was demolished in 1971 to make way for a very much larger and more modern centre. The building on the left, at the corner of Tottenham Court Road and Oxford Street used to be a Lyon's Corner House, built in 1923. These establishments, of which there were at least two others in London, consisted of a number of different restaurants which offered good food at low prices because of catering on a large scale.

London, Oxford Circus and Oxford Street.

90. Reference has already been made to Oxford Street as the busiest of London's shopping streets. After Tottenham Court and Charing Cross Roads its main junction before Marble Arch (cf. card No. 53) is with Regent Street, running down to the south to Piccadilly Circus (cf. card No. 58). This card shows that junction which is known as Oxford Circus. The road running north from the Circus contains Broadcasting House, the headquarters of the B.B.C. (cf. card No. 9). Buses with covered tops (that about to cross the Circus is on route 25) and a variety of motor vehicles are beginning to appear. There are likewise very many pedestrians, although nothing like the number likely to be found in this area today. Most of the main chain stores have their central London branches in Oxford Street.

THAMES EMBANKMENT, LONDON.

LP. 416.

95. The view on this card, published by Lansdowne Production Co., London, is very similar to that on card No. 41, apart from the fact that Hotel Cecil, the large building towards the right, has been demolished and in its place is Shell-Mex House, opened in 1933. Its tower rises to over 200 feet, and contains the largest clock in London. The Strand entrance to Hotel Cecil can be seen on the cover picture. It will also be seen from the card that motor vehicles have now taken over completely from those of the horse-drawn variety. Gone, too, are the single-deck trams which used to run to and from North London through the Kingsway Subway (cf. card No. 88) before it was enlarged in the early 1930s. The line 33 double-decker on the card used to run from West Norwood in South London to Manor House in North London. London's last tram ran in July 1952, the two routes using Kingsway subway being amongst the last to be abandoned. Part of the tunnel is now used for road traffic.

Brondesbury Road, Kilburn

96. Cards of streets in London suburban residential districts are not very common, this making the present example in Valentine's series all the more interesting and welcome. It is a view of Brondesbury Road in Kilburn in north-west London looking in the direction of Kilburn High Road into which Brondesbury Road runs. This is one of the many areas in London which developed more or less rapidly from the middle of the 19th century, not least as a result of rail links with the City and West End. Turning to the card we find substantial brick houses with pleasant trees lining the road, a few horse-drawn vehicles, and several children and adults walking along the footpath. It would seem that one of the houses on the left has a for-sale board outside it. There is also a church, which is still standing today, further along the street on the right in the direction of Kilburn High Road. It is also interesting to note that hardly any of the street scenes in this book show any litter in the streets and certainly no griffiti on buildings. It is no wonder that many people like to look back on the past with a real sense of nostalgia.

The Welsh Harp.
8503   Hendon.

97. The point was made in the Introduction that London is in effect the result of a coalescence of a number of more or less isolated villages. This is well illustrated by this card which shows a view of the 'Welsh Harp' at Hendon. This old alehouse stood on the Edgware Road, very near the junction of that part of it known as the Broadway and the North Circular Road on the borders of Hendon, Willesden and Kingsbury, a little to the north-east of Wembley Stadium. As can be seen from this card, the whole area was distinctly rural in the Edwardian era whereas it is today an extremely busy residential district, albeit it very well provided with open spaces and sports grounds. The name of the 'Welsh Harp' also lives on as an alternative name for Brent Reservoir which is to the left of Edgware Road. Both the public house and reservoir were very popular places of recreation and entertainment from about 1860 to 1910. They also figure in Victorian music-hall songs.

2. High Street. Barnet.

98. Barnet is still very much on the northern edge of London proper, at least as far as London as a continuous built-up area is concerned. The district had for very many years been on the main road to the north out of London and was important when coaches were still the main means of long-distance transport. In common with other outlying parts of London, its population increased greatly with the coming of the railways. This card, postally used in November 1909, shows the scene at the top of High Street in Barnet. Note the number of bicycles, the horse-drawn cart being led on the right and the lady pushing what would seem to be two prams! The tram, operated by Metropolitan Electric Tramways Co., which had many lines in north London at that time, is bound for Highgate (cf. card No. 99). It is interesting to note that even in this relatively quiet part of London it was found necessary to put up outside the church a notice reading 'Please pass the Church quietly'! Barnet had a large number of inns because of its fair and market. There is one – The Old Bull Inn – next to Berrill's Bazaar on the right of the card.

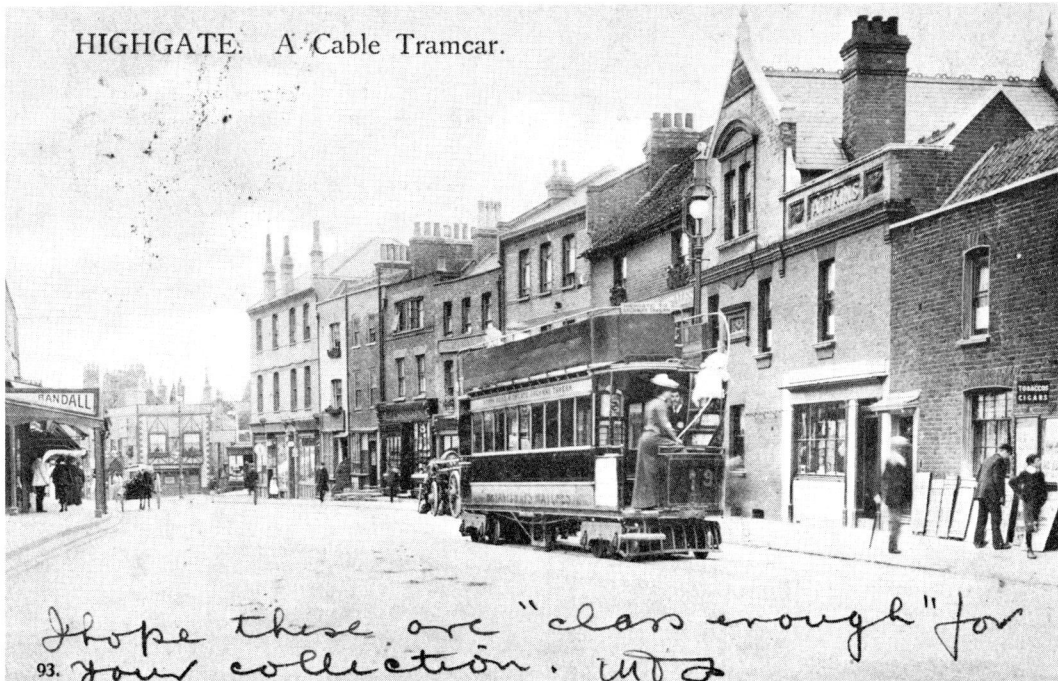

HIGHGATE. A Cable Tramcar.

I hope these are "class enough" for your collection. MD

93.

99. The destination of the tram shown on the previous card was Highgate, a fashionable suburb lying slightly to the north of Hampstead (cf. card No. 32). A very steep road leads from Highgate village down to Archway Tavern. It is crossed by the bridge of Hornsey Lane. Because of the steep gradient it was considered safer to use a cable tram on this stretch. It was the only cable line in North London and ran from 1884 to 1909. The card, published by Charles Martin, well known for his scenes in London suburbs, was postally used in July 1904. It shows an excellent view of one of the open-top cable cars used on the route with a child followed by a smartly dressed lady making their way to the top deck. Note the shop selling 'tobaccos' and cigars on the right and the relative peace and quiet of the whole scene.

HIGHBURY. — Upper Street.

100. Postally used in November 1903, this card, published by Charles Martin, well known for his cards of suburban London in Edwardian times, shows a view of Upper Street near Highbury Corner in north London. Of special interest on it is the horse tram about to begin its journey to Moorgate. London's last horse tram did not in fact cease running until 1915, although most former horse lines had been replaced by electric trams well before then. Note, too, the men standing outside 'The Cock Tavern' and the two fine lamps attached to the front of the building. Upper Street is today a very much busier thoroughfare than it was when this card was published. Its continuation in a northerly direction is Holloway Road.

Plaistow   The Barking Road (near the „Abbey Arms")

101. Postally used in September 1909, the product of a local publisher, this card presents a good idea of the multitude of activities going on at various levels in an East London street in the latter years of Edward VII's reign. The picture features an electric tram, at least one horse bus, various other horse-drawn vehicles, well dressed gentlemen and poorly dressed children, and artisans of various types. The scene is of Barking Road in that part of London known as Plaistow. The public house near the corner on the right of the card is the 'Abbey Arms'. Not only did pubs play a significant part in Victorian and Edwardian social life, but they were also important landmarks in locating places.

15672 BARKING ROAD.   EAST HAM.

102. This card also shows a further street scene in Barking Road, somewhat to the north-east of that shown on the preceding card. Postally used early in January 1910, we see three types of vehicles side by side, namely (from left to right) a horse-drawn dray, an electric tram, and a horse bus. Note the variety of containers and implements hanging from the back of the dray, some at least of these no doubt being intended to accommodate the horse's droppings. Although there is none visible in the street, there are two shops advertising cycles, that on the right being next to a branch of a well-known firm of cash chemists. The tall building on the right is East Ham Town Hall. Note that there are overhead wires for trams to collect their current, use being made of the elaborate lamp posts to support them. The destination of the electric tram is Green Street in Bethnal Green, this also being the destination of the card.

EAST INDIA DOCK ROAD, LOOKING EAST.

103. This locally produced card shows yet another typical street scene in London's East End, on this occasion in East India Dock Road, fairly near to the Blackwall Tunnel (cf. card No. 18). This part of London is known as Poplar. Note, once again, the variety of horse-drawn vehicles, and an electric tram with Aldgate, at the border between the City and East End, as its destination. Caps seem to be the standard headgear for the working-class men on the card, while some of the younger girls are wearing attractive hats or bonnets. The bakery of William Theis on the left also features the name of a well-known bread manufacturer of today.

GRAMMAR SCHOOL, TOOLEY STREET S.E.

104. For the remaining street scenes in our book we cross to the south of London's river. Tooley Street begins at the southern end of London bridge (cf. card No. 2) and runs eastwards more or less parallel to the Thames as far as Tower bridge (cf. card No. 1). The view of the street on this card, printed in Germany and therefore predating World War One, is very near Tower Bridge Road. There is on the left the impressive grammar school building. Note the horse-drawn bus and the various other horse-drawn vehicles. This area of London today gives the impression of having seen better days and the appearance of some of the human figures on the card suggests that this may well have been true.

Elephant and Castle.

105. The important part played in Victorian and Edwardian London by public houses has already been referred to (cf. card No. 101). The Elephant and Castle was originally a smithy, but was converted to a tavern in about 1760. The area has always constituted a notorious traffic junction, part of the confusion at which has in recent years been alleviated by the use of traffic signals. This card shows a view of the junction in about 1907. Note the variety of horse-drawn vehicles, including buses, and the three open-topped electric trams. One of the few elements of this view still standing today is the railway bridge across Newington Causeway which can be seen in the left background. Virtually everything else has changed during the past eighty years, not necessarily for the better!

STREATHAM. HIGH ROAD.

E.T.W.D.

106. Postally used in September 1906, this card in the 'Dainty' series of E.T.W. Dennis & Co., shows a delightful view of part of Streatham High Road in south-west London. This suburb has always been one of the more favoured as a residential area in South London and was yet another example of one which expanded immeasurably with the coming of the railway. Narrow and crowded as it may be, the shops and people in this section of the High Road confirm this impression of mid-Edwardian respectability. It is of interest that the signpost in the right foreground refers to the parts of South London covered by the remaining two cards, i.e. Balham and Croydon.

Nightingale Lane.

Balham.

107. This locally produced card, dating from the middle years of the reign of Edward VII, shows a quiet and dignified residential street, Nightingale Lane, in Balham (cf. card No. 96). This card illustrates well the point already made, i.e. that there are in London very different kinds of areas to be found bordering one another. The majority of the large family residences in this street will now have been let off as individual flats or bed-sitters. Sic transit gloria mundi! Part of Balham were bombed during World War Two. The suburb also contains some of South London's largest hospital complexes.

North End, Croydon

108. Some of London's tram routes were remarkably long, a good example being that which ran from the Embankment through south London to Purley. North of Purley is Croydon, and this Valentine card shows part of North End, its main thoroughfare in the direction of Purley. Note that, being so far from the centre of London, the tram can collect its current from overhead wires rather than via a plough suspended from the bottom of the tram through the road surface. Cycles, too, appear to have been popular. The shops seem well stocked, the goods in many cases having spread out onto the pavement, particularly on the left of the card. There will have been residential accommodation above most of the shops. The pedestrians, too, give the impression of being well dressed and fairly prosperous.